CITIZEN SCIENCE PROJECTS

Weather Projects

BY MATT LILLEY

Kids Core
An Imprint of Abdo Publishing
abdobooks.com

abdobooks.com

Printed in the United States of America, North Mankato, Minnesota.
102025
012026

THIS BOOK CONTAINS RECYCLED MATERIALS

Cover Photo: Shutterstock Images
Interior Photos: Shutterstock Images, 4–5, 6, 7, 9, 10, 18, 20–21, 24, 26, 29 (top), 29 (bottom); Budimir Jevtic/Shutterstock Images, 12–13; Doug McLean/Shutterstock Images, 14; John Kershner/Shutterstock Images, 15; Ivan Serebryannikov/Shutterstock Images, 17; Aleksey Sagitov/Shutterstock Images, 23; Sorapop Udomsri/Shutterstock Images, 28 (top); Steve Lovegrove/Shutterstock Images, 28 (bottom)

Editors: Rebecca Higgins and Trudy Becker
Series Designer: Marley Richmond

Library of Congress Control Number: 2025939192

Publisher's Cataloging-in-Publication Data

Names: Lilley, Matt, author.
Title: Weather projects / by Matt Lilley
Description: Minneapolis, Minnesota: Abdo Publishing, 2026 | Series: Citizen science projects | Includes online resources and index.
Identifiers: ISBN 9781098298609 (lib. bdg.) | ISBN 9798384932406 (ebook)
Subjects: LCSH: Science projects--Juvenile literature. | Field experiments--Juvenile literature. | Weather--Juvenile literature. | Weather--Experiments--Juvenile literature. | Meteorology--Juvenile literature. | Ecology--Experiments--Juvenile literature. | Ecological science--Juvenile literature.
Classification: DDC 507.8--dc23

CONTENTS

Dark clouds in the sky mean that the weather is changing. There is likely a storm on its way.

CHAPTER 1

A Tornado Tale

Kai was playing soccer with his friends in his backyard. Suddenly, the sky became dark. Kai and his friends ran into the house.

Then a loud siren blared. Kai knew the siren meant dangerous weather. His mom yelled, "Everyone in the basement!"

When there is severe weather, sirens sound to let people know to take shelter.

They rushed to a room in the basement with no windows. It was the safest place.

Kai's mom got a weather alert on her phone. She told them there was a tornado warning. This meant that a tornado had been seen in the area. They needed to wait in the basement until the tornado was gone.

Outside, it stormed. Hail started falling. Tree branches scraped against the house. Eventually, the storm passed. Kai's mom checked her phone again. "The warning is over," she said. "We can go back upstairs."

A tornado is a rotating column of air that sometimes touches the ground. People should take shelter during a tornado warning.

They looked out the window. Some trees had fallen. But they were all safe.

After his friends went home, Kai turned on the computer. He knew about a citizen science project for tornadoes. The **survey** was called Tornado Tales. Kai worked with his mom to describe their experience. They answered questions about whether they received a

Watch or Warning?

A tornado watch means that a tornado might form. A tornado warning means that there is a tornado in an area. It has been seen by a person or detected by radar. Radar sends out energy called radio waves. The waves bounce off objects such as clouds. That tells scientists what kind of weather is happening.

People participating in Tornado Tales must be 18 years old or older, but children can help a trusted adult complete the survey.

tornado warning and what they did when they heard the siren. Scientists use the survey to understand what people do when there is a tornado. They want to learn how to keep people safe during these storms.

Citizen scientists record weather data and share it with researchers.

Citizen Science for Weather

Citizen science projects let everyone be a part of scientific research. Citizen scientists collect **data**. Scientists use this information to learn more about certain topics, including weather. Weather is the state of the air in one place and time. Temperature, wind, **precipitation**, clouds, **humidity**, and more all make up the weather. The weather constantly changes. There is a lot of data, and scientists need help collecting it.

Scientists work to better understand the weather. Citizen scientists help collect weather data. With more data, scientists can make better **predictions**.

Explore Online

Look at the website below. Does it give any new information about weather?

Weather

abdocorelibrary.com/weather-projects

Some people may track precipitation for a citizen science project. Others may track it to know how much to water their plants.

CHAPTER 2

Backyard Weather

There are many ways people can help with citizen science projects. One project is the Community Collaborative Rain, Hail, and Snow Network (CoCoRaHS). Volunteers for CoCoRaHS track precipitation. They measure rain, snow, and hail.

Manual rain gauges track precipitation best when they are placed in open areas.

Volunteers send a quick application to join. Kids can apply with the help of a parent or guardian. For this project, citizen scientists need a manual rain gauge with a diameter of 4 inches (10 cm) or 8 inches (20 cm).

After a brief training, volunteers set up their rain gauges. Citizen scientists check the gauges every day at the same time. It is best to check them in the morning. Then volunteers record on the website how much precipitation there was. They even record if there wasn't any. This information still helps scientists.

CoCoRaHS volunteers also track snow and hail. A flat board and a ruler are used to measure snow. The ruler should measure to one-tenth of an inch. New snow is measured soon after it snows. A storm with hail is severe weather. Volunteers report hail right away.

Citizen scientists can measure how much snow has fallen by reading the number closest to the top of the snow.

Lots of groups use CoCoRaHS's data. **Meteorologists** use it for flood warnings and weather predictions. Farmers use the data to decide how much to water their crops.

Tracking the Weather

Some citizen scientists set up an entire weather station. Cooperative Observer Program (COOP)

Looking Up

Meteorological Phenomena Identification Near the Ground (mPING) is a citizen science project. Scientists use radar and **satellites** to track the weather. However, these tools can't see what's happening on the ground. Volunteers can track the current weather on an app called mPING. Scientists compare these ground reports with other data.

Weather stations can include wind vanes. These instruments tell people which direction the wind is blowing.

volunteers check their weather stations every day. They report the daily high and low temperatures. They record how deep the snow is. They might collect other data too.

Volunteers for GLOBE Clouds report on cloud cover. They report what kinds of clouds they see. They take pictures. Scientists compare the cloud data to **satellite** images. This helps them understand information from their satellites.

Tools to Measure the Weather

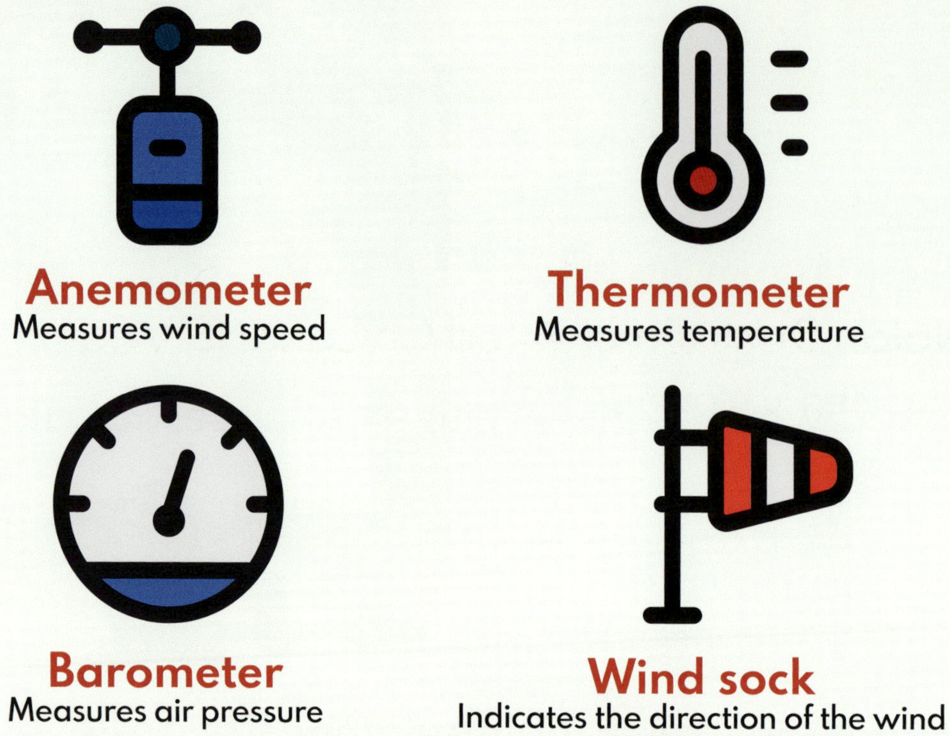

There are many weather tools that citizen scientists can use. They each measure a different part of the weather.

Scientists can see what the satellite shows and what that looks like from the ground. Clouds can make a hot day cooler. They are part of the weather, but they also change it. Tracking clouds helps scientists predict the weather.

Primary Source

Nolan Doesken created CoCoRaHS. When asked why he enjoys citizen science, he said:

> I've always been thrilled by weather and climate. To have the chance to share that and see the same excitement grow in thousands of others is just the best feeling.

Source: Sarah Newman. "Interview with Nolan Doesken, CSA Board Member & CoCoRaHS Director." *Association for Advancing Participatory Sciences*, 8 Oct. 2015, participatorysciences.org. Accessed 23 Feb. 2025.

Point of View

Read this quote carefully. What is the speaker's point of view on weather and citizen science? What is your point of view? Write a short essay about how they are the same or different.

Weather is temporary. Climate describes the usual weather conditions for an area.

CHAPTER 3

Weather and Climate

Weather and climate are related. The weather describes what is happening at a certain time. The weather one day might be rainy, but the next day it could be sunny. The climate is what happens over a long time, such as if a place is usually warm.

To understand climate better, scientists need information over a long period of time. They need old data. People have been recording the weather for hundreds of years. Those records are in old logs and notebooks. Volunteers enter that data into computers so it's easier for scientists to use.

Irish Weather Rescue records old data. Ireland's National Weather Service has weather records going back to 1855. It has

Meteorology

Meteorology is the study of the weather. The word *meteor* comes from a Greek word that means "things in the sky." In ancient Greece, anything in the sky was called a meteor.

Sailors tracked the weather in their logs and notebooks.

3.5 million rainfall records. That data can help researchers understand Ireland's climate.

Sailors have kept weather logs for hundreds of years. Citizen scientists read their logs. Then they enter the data online.

Some volunteers for Fresh Eyes on Ice collect information about ice on rivers.

Changing Climate

Earth's climate is changing. Scientists use weather data to understand these changes. It helps them predict the future climate.

The climate is changing faster in the Arctic than in other places. Scientists want to protect the Arctic, but they need to know more about ice. In Fresh Eyes on Ice, volunteers in Alaska and other parts of North America observe and track ice on rivers and lakes. Scientists use this information to learn more about the Arctic and its climate.

A few people take their commitment to citizen science to the next level. Two women started a major citizen science project in 2019. They spent 18 months living on Svalbard, a group of islands in Norway. They tracked the snow and sea ice. The volunteers flew a drone that gathered weather data. They also helped measure the size of the glaciers there.

Two citizen scientists, Hilde Fålun Strøm and Sunniva Sorby, stayed in this cabin in Norway while collecting data.

They took pictures of auroras and clouds. The volunteers collected data for eight research groups.

At the time, COVID-19 was spreading and scientists were unable to travel. They would not have been able to get that information without citizen scientists. This data helps scientists better understand the climate.

Citizen scientists collect data in many different ways. They help researchers learn more about weather. These volunteers make a difference in people's everyday lives.

Further Evidence

Watch the video at the website below. Does it give any new evidence to support Chapter Three?

Weather vs. Climate

abdocorelibrary.com/weather-projects

Science Projects

Volunteers who are reporting their experience with a tornado online need to be 18 years of age or older. Kids may help a trusted adult with the project.

Citizen scientists who are tracking rainfall need a rain gauge. They may need a specific gauge depending on the project.

People who are recording snowfall totals need a board or other flat surface and a ruler that meets the project requirements.

Citizen scientists who are tracking ice on rivers and lakes may need a camera.

Glossary

data
information

humidity
the amount of water in the air

meteorologists
people who study the weather

precipitation
water that returns to Earth, such as rain or snow

predictions
guesses about what will happen in the future

satellite
a human-made or natural object that orbits a larger body in space

survey
a series of questions used to collect information

Online Resources

To learn more about weather projects, visit our free resource websites below.

Core Library
CONNECTION
FREE! COMMON CORE MULTIMEDIA RESOURCES

Visit **abdocorelibrary.com** or scan this QR code for free Common Core resources for teachers and students, including vetted activities, multimedia, and booklinks, for deeper subject comprehension.

Booklinks
NONFICTION NETWORK
FREE! ONLINE NONFICTION RESOURCES

Visit **abdobooklinks.com** or scan this QR code for free additional online weblinks for further learning. These links are routinely monitored and updated to provide the most current information available.

Learn More

Buckey, A.W. *Weather.* Abdo, 2025.

Olson, Elsie. *Meteorology Lab: Explore Weather with Art & Activities.* Abdo, 2024.

Setford, Steve. *Why? Weather.* DK, 2024.

Index

About the Author

Matt Lilley has an MS in scientific and technical writing. The focus of his degree was on medical writing for kids. He loves researching and writing about all sorts of topics. He lives in Minnesota with his family.